ALLYN & BACON
VideoWorkshop
A COURSE TAILORED VIDEO LEARNING SYSTEM

Family Therapy
Student Learning Guide
with CD-ROM

Michael P. Nichols
College of William and Mary

PEARSON

Boston   New York San Francisco
Mexico City Montreal Toronto London Madrid Munich Paris
Hong Kong Singapore Tokyo Cape Town Sydney

Copyright © 2006 Pearson Education, Inc.

All rights reserved. No part of the material protected by this copyright notice may be reproduced or utilized in any form or by any means, electronic or mechanical, including photocopying, recording, or by any information storage and retrieval system, without written permission from the copyright owner.

To obtain permission(s) to use material from this work, please submit a written request to Allyn and Bacon, Permissions Department, 75 Arlington Street, Boston, MA 02116 or fax your request to 617-848-7320.

ISBN 0-205-46283-9

Printed in the United States of America

10 9 8 7 6 5   10 09

Allyn and Bacon Video Workshop: Family Therapy

Preface

This Student Learning Guide accompanies the *Allyn & Bacon Video Workshop for Marriage and Family Therapy*. It is designed to enhance your experience with the videos.

Features:

- **General Questions** (page 3) help you to think about the "big picture" of family therapy as you observe the videos showing the various schools of family therapy on the enclosed CD.
- **Brief Synopsis** of situation.
- **Observation Questions** focus on the video itself.

Allyn and Bacon Video Workshop: Family Therapy

Table of Contents

General Overview..3

Video 1: Bowenian Therapy with Dr. Phil Guerin...4

Video 2: Feminist Therapy with Dr. Cheryl Rampage...8

Video 3: Values-Sensitive Family Therapy with Dr. Bill Doherty.......................11

Video 4: Culture-Sensitive Therapy with Dr. Jon Carlson and Dr. Mary Arnold.................16

Video 5: Internal Family Systems Therapy with Richard Schwartz.....................19

Video 6: Satir Therapy with Jean McLendon...23

Video 7: Experiential Therapy with Dr. Gus Napier..26

Video 8: Behavioral Therapy with Dr. Richard Stuart...29

Video 9: Structural Therapy with Dr. Harry J. Aponte..33

Video 10: Sex Therapy with Dr. Domeena Renshaw...37

Video 11: Strategic Therapy with Dr. James Coyne..41

Video 12: Solution-Oriented Therapy with Bill O'Hanlon..................................46

Video 13: Object Relations Therapy with Drs. David and Jill Scharff................51

Video 14: Narrative Therapy with Dr. Steve Madigan..56

Video 15: Integrative Family Therapy with Dr. Ken Hardy................................61

Video 16: Imago Therapy with Dr. Pat Love...67

Video 17: Empowerment Family Therapy with Dr. Frank Pittman....................73

Video 18: Adlerian Therapy with Dr. James Bitter...80

Video 19: Emotionally Focused Couples with Dr. Susan Johnson.....................85

General Overview

Each of the segments selected from the tapes in this series illustrates certain features of various schools of family therapy. Each illustrates particular points and raises specific questions. There are also general questions that you might ask about all of these interviews.

General Questions:

1. How effectively does the therapist join with the clients? How is this accomplished?

2. How effectively does the therapist rejoin with clients when necessary – as for example when a patient gets angry or feels misunderstood?

3. How effectively does the therapist get a clear picture of the presenting complaint? (This may be hard to determine when watching only selected segments of certain tapes.)

4. How effectively does the therapist focus on solving the presenting complaint?

5. How effectively does the therapist uncover what various family members are doing to maintain the presenting complaint?

6. How effectively does the therapist uncover *why* family members are doing what they do to maintain the presenting problem?

7. How effectively does the therapist focus on the process of interaction between family members?

8. How effectively does the therapist focus on the family's structure?

9. Does the therapist's assessment of what the client(s) should do seem to be uncovered from an understanding of their unique situation or does it seem to be imposed from the therapist's general approach?

10. To what extent is the therapist guilty of acting as though problems are easily solved?

11. How would you approach this interview differently?

Allyn and Bacon Video Workshop: Family Therapy

Bowenian Therapy with Dr. Phil Guerin

Brief Synopsis:

This family in this consultation consists of a husband and wife and 32-year-old daughter who lives at home. The presenting complaint is that the daughter doesn't listen to her parents. She is dependent on them, but the price of that is that they are always full of criticism and advice. When she feels pushed, she retreats into silence or says "I don't know." Thus, her "not listening" is really a symptom of the rebellion of an adult child enmeshed with her controlling parents.

Segment 2-1 – 2-2 The father, Adrian, says they've had problems with their daughter Pam for years. She doesn't answer them when they try to talk to her. Then he turns to Pam and asks, "What else?" She doesn't answer.

Observation Questions:

1. What does the seating arrangement and who is talking about whom suggest is the primary emotional triangle in this family?

_____
_____
_____
_____
_____
_____
_____
_____

Segment 2-10 – 2-14 Both parents agree that Pam is closer to her father. The mother has tried to do things with Pam but Pam just seems to avoid her. When asked why this is so, Pam doesn't really say much. The father comes in to say that he has tried to push them together, but it hasn't done much good.

Observation Questions:

1. Why is Pam (the daughter) closer to her father than to her mother?

2. What contributions do each of the three family members make to the perpetuation of this triangle?

3. What protective functions (for all 3 family members) does the triangle in this family serve?

Allyn and Bacon Video Workshop: Family Therapy

Segment 2-24 – 2-26 *In this segment, Guerin asks the daughter if her parents get upset that she doesn't have more of a social life. She says, as she often does, "I don't know," but they have told her so and they have made many suggestions about how she should develop more of a social life.*

Observation Questions:

1. What does Pam's saying "I don't know" mean?

_____
_____
_____
_____
_____
_____
_____
_____

2. Why did she develop the defensive maneuver, and how effective is it?

_____
_____
_____
_____
_____
_____

3. Why isn't she able to be more directly assertive? That is, what price would she have to pay to do so? What holds her back?

_____
_____
_____
_____

4. How, as a therapist, might you help her be more direct?

5. Does Pam's retreat into silence remind you of anyone else in the family?

Allyn and Bacon Video Workshop: Family Therapy

Feminist Therapy with Dr. Cheryl Rampage

Brief Synopsis:

This consultation is with feminist family therapist Cheryl Rampage and a single mother and her six-year-old son. The mother sees herself as a failure and her son as having lots of problems. The boy isn't doing well in school, he doesn't do his homework, and he is going to be held back a year. The mother feels guilty about having a broken marriage and wonders if her son might be depressed because his father isn't around.

Segment 2-15 – 2-16 In this segment the 6-year-old describes how he gives his mother regular foot massages and back rubs.

Observation Questions:

1. Why might a structural family therapist interpret this as evidence of enmeshment? What relevance would this interpretation have understanding the boy's performing poorly in school and not doing his homework?

2. How might a feminist offer an alternative interpretation (to enmeshment) for this behavior? What relevance would this interpretation have for understanding the boy's performing poorly in school and not doing his homework?

3. Does a therapist show more respect for a mother by praising her or by asking her how she feels about the situation?

Segment 2-43 *In summing up, Dr. Rampage tells the mother that both she and her son are working hard to be a good family. Moreover, Dr. Rampage tells her that maybe she has no need to feel so guilty and insecure about the job she's doing as a single mother. In the process, as throughout the interview, Dr. Rampage does not comment on the presenting problem – the boy's poor school performance.*

Observation Questions:

1. Is the therapist merely offering bland support without any explanation or solution for the boy's problems in school?

2. Discuss the validity of a feminist analysis of this situation which might say that the underlying problem is the mother's self-doubt and lack of support for her role as a single mother, and that by pointing out the mother's heroic accomplishments the therapist is supporting her in a way that will help her to do a better job of helping her son succeed in school.

Allyn and Bacon Video Workshop: Family Therapy

Values-Sensitive Family Therapy with Dr. Bill Doherty

Brief Synopsis:

The client in this session is a married woman who has been having an affair. She is trying to decide whether to leave her husband or end the affair. Dr. Doherty urges the woman to think about the consequences for others of her decision. He also suggests that rather than chose between leaving her family or staying in a loveless marriage there is a third possibility: to stay in the marriage but make an effort to revitalize it. He also suggests that only by confessing her affair to her husband could she make an honest attempt to bring more intimacy to her marriage.

Segment 2-20 – 2-24 *In this segment Doherty asks the client to consider what the consequences of her staying in or leaving the marriage might be for her husband and her children, rather than simply which choice might lead to greater personal happiness for herself.*

Observation Questions:

1. Is the impact of Doherty's interventions to get the woman to think about her options and their consequences, or is it really a thinly disguised suggestion?

    _____
    _____
    _____
    _____
    _____
    _____
    _____
    _____

2. Consider the possibility that this client is wrestling with a conflict (leave or stay) that she has been unable to resolve, and she projects into the consultant the decision that she wants him to make for her. What evidence can you marshal to suggest that the woman gets Doherty to say what she wants him to say?

    _____
    _____

Allyn and Bacon Video Workshop: Family Therapy

3. What assumptions are implicit in the idea that this woman should break off her affair and recommit herself to her marriage?

4. Can you think of a more balanced way for a therapist to help this woman think about her options?

5. What are the implications of a male consultant telling a(n apparently passive) female client what to do?

Segment 2-30 – 2-33 In this segment Doherty suggests to the client that she should confess to her husband that she has been having an affair as a precondition to putting the marriage back on an honest footing.

Observation Questions:

1. What assumptions are implicit in this suggestion? What are some alternative possibilities?

2. In what way is the consultant relieving the client of the burden of making her own decisions?

Allyn and Bacon Video Workshop: Family Therapy

3. In terms of psychodynamic structures (id, ego, superego), what side of the client's conflict is the consultant taking? What parts of her psyche are then pushed aside? If she follows the consultant's advice, what might be the consequences in these terms?

___

4. What are the possible consequences of a married woman confessing to her husband that she's had an affair?

___

5. Are husbands or wives more likely to seek a divorce in response to their partner's having an affair?

___

6. Discuss the possibility that this client knows that she should leave her husband for the man she loves but has been holding back due to neurotic inhibitions.

7. What role might gender play in a consultant's decision to give advice, and the client's deciding to take it?

Allyn and Bacon Video Workshop: Family Therapy

Culture-Sensitive Therapy with Dr. Jon Carlson and Dr. Mary Arnold

Brief Synopsis:

The clients in this consultation are John and Martha, a couple in their forties both married for the second time. The presenting problem is that they fight about handling their respective fourteen-year-old children. "The kids are pulling us apart." In particular, Martha thinks John should be more forceful in insisting that his fourteen-year-old son visit more frequently.

Segment 2-17 – 2-20 In this segment Dr. Arnold asks the couple what are their ethnic backgrounds. The husband says, "I'm Polish, if that means anything," and the wife says that she is part Irish, part [?], and part Native American. Dr. Arnold suggests that the husband's Polish background and the wife's Irish background may be important in shaping how they approach family relationships.

Observation Questions:

1. How does the introduction of the clients' ethnic backgrounds facilitate problem solving in this case?

_____
_____
_____
_____
_____
_____
_____

2. Are the traits that the therapists impute to Polish and Irish people, respectively, things they've observed in the clients or are they cultural stereotypes?

_____
_____

3. What clues do you have about the couple's involvement with their extended families, and what relevance might this have for their current difficulties?

Segment 2-25 – 2-27 *In this segment, Martha says that John should get tougher and insist that his fourteen-year-old son visit more regularly. He listens without saying much, as though he's heard this many times before. Mary Arnold suggests that this get-tough approach might work for "a strong Irish woman," but that it doesn't work for "a Polish man."*

Observation Questions:

1. In what ways does attributing the clients' differing positions to their ethnic backgrounds help foster understanding?

2. What is the classic triangle involved in this instance, a wife urging her husband to get tougher with his ex, and how well do you think it's addressed?

3. What is the process by which the couple handles their disagreements? What is the family structure involved?

Allyn and Bacon Video Workshop: Family Therapy

Internal Family Systems Therapy with Richard Schwartz

Brief Synopsis:

The clients in this interview are a married couple in their late thirties. They've been working on their relationship in therapy, but he wants "some information on how to enhance their relationship," and she wants to figure out how some of her problems in the present relate to her childhood. She wishes he did more around the house but doesn't feel that he's willing to accept her making complaints. When she gets angry with him, he feels threatened and abandoned, which in turn makes him pull away. Thus, she feels punished for expressing her needs and is now afraid to do so. Dr. Schwartz helps the couple re-imagine their conflicts as due not to basic incompatibilities but to defensive "parts" of themselves getting activated and making them attack or withdraw from each other out of fear.

Segment 2-25 – 2-31 With Dr. Schwartz's help, the wife imagines the "part" of her who is afraid to open up (and complain) to her husband as a frightened little girl, afraid that she'll be punished for expressing her feelings. Thus she begins to see her fear of opening up as something that is, at least in part, coming from inside of herself, not just a reaction to her husband.

Observation Questions:

1. What is the effect of the consultant's asking the wife to think about her fear of opening up to her husband as due to a fearful "part" of herself (rather than as something he does)?

_____
_____
_____
_____
_____
_____
_____

Allyn and Bacon Video Workshop: Family Therapy

2. What about the consultant's demeanor helps makes this exploration safe for the woman?

3. What effect does the consultant's exploration of the wife's fearful little girl "part" have on the husband's ability to understand what his wife is feeling? What makes him less defensive about this?

4. Is there any extent to which the conversation about "masks" and "being afraid to express feelings" blurs the distinction between talking about feelings and complaining about the husband's behavior?

Allyn and Bacon Video Workshop: Family Therapy

Segment 2-37 – 2-41 *After the wife has finished crying about the little girl inside her who is afraid to talk about her feelings, Dr. Schwartz asks her husband for his reaction. When he says that he wants her to open up, Dr. Schwartz reminds him that it is his own tendency to pull away from her when she complains that makes her afraid to open up. The husband accepts this interpretation and agrees to work on not pulling away from her.*

Observation Questions:

1. What function might the husband's apparently overoptimistic response serve?

2. What are the various Internal Family System's terms for subpersonalities (e.g., parts, firefighters, etc.) and what do they mean? How do these personifications help people understand and resolve their conflicts?

3. What is the most effective thing (or things) the consultant achieves in these two segments? What do you think might have been overlooked? How would you advance the work begun in these segments using the Internal Family Systems model?

_____
_____
_____
_____
_____
_____
_____
_____

Allyn and Bacon Video Workshop: Family Therapy

Satir Therapy with Jean McLendon

Brief Synopsis:

Eleven-year-old Jonathan asked his mother to help him find a counselor to help him deal with his anger. His mother complied and this interview with Jean McLendon is the result. In the interview McLendon uncovers a series of losses in the boy's life and interprets his anger as his way of defending against feelings of sadness. "Underneath a lot of anger," she tells the boy, "is a hurt. There is a little boy inside of you, and he's been hurt." McLendon then helps the mother to cry about the recent loss of her own mother. Following this she turns to the boy and asks him to hold a stuffed puppy to symbolize the sad little boy inside of him. The boy accepts the puppy and seems willing to accept that he should be more sympathetic to his own feelings of loss and sadness.

Segment 2-20 – 2-26 McLendon talks about all the losses the boy has suffered, including the death of his grandmother, his parents' divorce, and his older brother's incarceration. She asks him to hold a stuffed puppy and tells him that he has to reassure the puppy that it's okay to be sad. Thus, she interprets the boy's anger as the result of his trying to cover up his pain over the losses he has suffered.

McLendon also works briefly with the mother, offering her a doll to hold which she says can symbolize the hurt little girl inside of her.

Observation Questions:

1. How does the boy seem to respond to the interpretation that his anger is a mask for grief?

_____
_____
_____
_____
_____
_____
_____

Allyn and Bacon Video Workshop: Family Therapy

2. What other possible sources of the boy's anger can you think of?

_____
_____
_____
_____
_____
_____
_____
_____

3. Do you think the consultant does a good job of considering the interpersonal context of the boy's feelings?

_____
_____
_____
_____
_____
_____
_____
_____

4. What suggestions are there that the boy and his mother are enmeshed following the mother's divorce and loss of her own mother and her failure to make new adult connections?

_____
_____
_____
_____
_____
_____
_____
_____

5. What role might the mother's close relationship with her pre-adolescent son have in his feelings of anger?

6. How effectively does catharsis of his sadness help this eleven-year-old boy deal with his feelings of anger?

7. Does the fact that this mother and son are African-American make any difference in this session, and should it?

Allyn and Bacon Video Workshop: Family Therapy

Experiential Therapy with Dr. Gus Napier

Brief Synopsis:

Bill (47) and Pat (50) have been living together for three years, but their increasingly angry arguments have them on the verge of splitting up. Pat complains that Bill shuts her out by not sharing things with her, while he feels that she badgers him. Among the stresses on their relationship are Bill's recent heart attack and financial troubles subsequent to Pat's having been out of work.

Segment 2-15 – 2-26, but delete the middle part, 2-21 – 2-22, in which the therapist talks to Pat. Pat admits that she has a terrible temper, and she realizes that this is a dangerous stress on Bill's heart. Napier interprets Pat's behavior as parental and controlling, and Bill's response as passive-aggressive withdrawal.

Observation Questions:

1. How effectively has the consultant made the couple feel safe enough to tolerate his confrontation?

_____
_____
_____
_____
_____
_____
_____

2. Which of the partners seems to accept Napier's interpretations, and why?

_____
_____
_____
_____

3. How does Bill's experiences in childhood relate to his response to Pat?

4. What might help to explain Pat's powerful response to being shut out?

Segment 2-37 – 2-40 *Napier catches Bill smiling when Pat talks about his mocking her, and he confronts Bill for goading her into attacking him.*

Observation Questions:

1. How would the hypothesis that Pat's anger is a response to feelings of abandonment fit with her response to Bill and her experience growing up?

Allyn and Bacon Video Workshop: Family Therapy

2. What evidence is there that Bill fear's engulfment? What in his past might help to explain this? Can you think of an alternative hypothesis?

3. How much support can you adduce to support the notion that Pat's rage and Bill's almost aggressive passivity have homicidal and suicidal overtones (giving his serious cardiac condition)?

Allyn and Bacon Video Workshop: Family Therapy

Behavioral Therapy with Dr. Richard Stuart

Brief Synopsis:

Wesley and Adele are a middle-aged, working-class couple. This is her third marriage and his fourth. Wesley feels rejected because Adele frequently works late, and she feels that he isn't affectionate with her and doesn't show her that he cares for her. The interview is a very structured one in which Dr. Stuart begins with a brief family history with each spouse and then explores the history of their relationship with each other. In the second half of the interview, Dr. Stuart offers the couple suggestions for improving their relationship by making an effort to act "as if" things were good and they cared for each other.

Segment 2-26 – 2-32 Dr. Stuart tells the couple that they can choose to make their marriage work by acting in loving ways toward each other. They both seem a little skeptical, and Adele reveals that she doesn't know if Wesley is committed to staying in the relationship. Stuart suggests that she needs to feel safe in his commitment and, using the example of his own marriage, tells them again that they can accentuate the positive by making a point of expressing their caring for each other.

Observation Questions:

1. To what extent to Dr. Stuart's suggestions seem tied to this couple's specific concerns versus being generic?

_____
_____
_____
_____
_____
_____
_____
_____

Allyn and Bacon Video Workshop: Family Therapy

2. Does Stuart seem to be ignoring the couple's conflicts? Is this necessarily a problem?

_____
_____
_____
_____
_____
_____
_____
_____
_____

3. To what extend does a learning need to explore how a couple's problems were learned?

_____
_____
_____
_____
_____
_____
_____
_____
_____
_____

Segment 2-35 – 2-37 *Stuart suggests that Wesley start acting "as if" he felt close to Adele and reassures him that if he acts affectionately, she will respond in kind. Again he uses his own marriage as an example of how two people can make themselves happy by making a point of acting lovingly toward each other. In fact, he guarantees Wesley that if he acts affectionately Adele will respond, and he asks Wesley to agree to try doing so as an experiment. Wesley agrees, somewhat skeptically.*

Observation Questions:

1. Does the couple seem to trust the therapist?

   _____
   _____
   _____
   _____
   _____
   _____
   _____

2. Do you think the couple would feel that the therapist understands their concerns?

   _____
   _____
   _____
   _____
   _____
   _____
   _____

3. In what ways do you think the therapist's tendency to give advice helpful? Not so helpful?

   _____
   _____
   _____
   _____
   _____
   _____
   _____

Allyn and Bacon Video Workshop: Family Therapy

4. Do you think the therapist was successful in promoting optimism? Can you think of any ways that he might have been more successful at doing so?

Allyn and Bacon Video Workshop: Family Therapy

Structural Family Therapy with Dr. Harry J. Aponte

Brief Synopsis:

This family in this consultation consists of a husband (Adrian) and wife (Judy) and 32-year-old daughter (Pam) who lives at home. The presenting complaint is that the daughter doesn't listen to her parents. She is dependent on them, but the price of that is that they are always full of criticism and advice. When she feels pushed, she retreats into silence or says "I don't know." Thus, her "not listening" is really a symptom of the rebellion of an adult child enmeshed with her controlling parents. (The same family was also interviewed by Philip Guerin in this video series.)

Segment 2-6 – 2-7 Aponte asks mom to find out why Pam is upset. (She's crying.) Pam says "I don't know."

Observation Questions:

1. How effective an example is this of enactment (the signal intervention in structural family therapy)?

2. What does this enactment reveal about the way the family relates to Pam?

Allyn and Bacon Video Workshop: Family Therapy

_____
_____
_____

3. What does this segment reveal about Pam's characteristic pattern of defensiveness?

_____
_____
_____
_____
_____
_____
_____
_____
_____

Segment 2-22 – 2-27 *Aponte focuses on a scene at breakfast as an illustration of the lack of connection between Pam and her mother. On weekends Pam typically sleeps later than her parents. When she comes to the kitchen too late for breakfast she usually gets mad but doesn't say anything. Aponte interprets this as evidence that she acts like a spoiled child. Moreover, he suggests that she doesn't want to grow up because she doesn't want to leave home. Later he asks her to agree to offer to help her mother cook breakfast, rather than merely pout when she doesn't get what she wants.*

Observation Questions:

1. What is the structural goal of Aponte's interventions?

_____
_____
_____
_____
_____
_____

2. How accurate is Aponte's interpretation that Pam doesn't want to work with her mother because she is spoiled?

3. What is Pam avoiding by not speaking up about what she wants for breakfast?

4. How likely is it that Pam will follow through on what she agrees to change? How as a therapist would you approach this issue in a subsequent session?

5. What is the father's role in the alienation between mother and daughter? What motivates this role? What might make it change?

_____
_____
_____
_____
_____
_____
_____

Allyn and Bacon Video Workshop: Family Therapy

Sex Therapy with Dr. Domeena Renshaw

Brief Synopsis:

This interview is with a twenty-eight-year-old wife and mother of a one-year-old whose husband refused to come at the last minute. Although the referral was because of the lack of sex between the couple since Jennifer became pregnant, it turns out that the marriage is in serious trouble. The young husband, who is currently out of work due to a job-related knee injury, stays out several nights a week drinking and presumably using cocaine. Jennifer has thought seriously about getting a divorce, but she is clearly ambivalent because she still loves her husband and has a lot invested in the relationship.

Segment 2-21 – 2-25 Dr. Renshaw asks Jennifer about her sexual history. She says that she was never abused, and that she had intercourse for the first time when she was fifteen. She and her husband had sex daily until she became pregnant at which point her husband stopped wanting to have sex with her. It's unclear how much this has to do with his drug abuse or with his reaction to his wife's becoming pregnant or to the couple's violent quarrels. Dr. Renshaw summarizes Jennifer's unstable family history. She suggests that Jennifer attend a few Al-Anon meetings to get some perspective on dealing with her husband's substance abuse.

Observation Questions:

1. What are the advantages and disadvantages of the interviewers asking so many specific questions (rather than smaller number of open-ended questions)?

___
___
___
___
___
___
___

Allyn and Bacon Video Workshop: Family Therapy

2. How neutral does the therapist remain?

_____
_____
_____
_____
_____
_____
_____

3. What pulls might an interviewer feel to push this young woman in a particular direction?

_____
_____
_____
_____
_____
_____
_____

Segment 2-37 – 2-43 *Dr. Renshaw sums up what Jennifer has said about her troubled marriage. Dr. Renshaw tries to articulate Jennifer's conflict over whether to divorce her husband. On the one hand, he seems to have a serious drug abuse problem, he's stopped showing any interest in sex, and he becomes violent during arguments. On the other hand, Jennifer still loves him and they have a house and a child together. Dr. Renshaw suggests that Jennifer stop her angry scolding when her husband comes home drunk, because that only seems to lead to escalating arguments. When Jennifer says that she should probably eventually leave her husband, Dr. Renshaw cautions her to make up her own mind and not be swayed by other people's advice.*

Observation Questions:

1. How well does the therapist support the patient's strengths?

2. How well does the therapist avoid taking a position about what the patient should do?

3. What are the pros and cons of staying neutral in this situation?

4. What are the possible reasons Jennifer's husband stopped having sex with her, and how would you explore these possibilities?

5. How effectively does the therapist avoid siding with the person in front of her against the person who isn't there? What are the consequences of siding with the person who is present against the person who is absent?

Allyn and Bacon Video Workshop: Family Therapy

Strategic Therapy with Dr. James Coyne

Brief Synopsis:

In this interview James Coyne meets with Alan and Hugh, a committed gay couple who have been together for twelve years. They are also partners in a landscaping business. The couple has recently come though a difficult and stressful period and, although, they are now getting along better they're still troubled by frequent minor arguments. Both partners see themselves as needing general suggestions to improve their relationship rather than as having any major problems at this time. Two issues emerge as minor, though persistent irritants. Hugh is bothered by the fact that Alan often expresses him self in vague and unclear ways and finds it difficult to understand or pin him down. Alan has trouble dealing with Hugh's anger. Even when Hugh expresses annoyance about something that has nothing to do with his partner, Alan gets upset and feels responsible.

Although this is couples therapy, Dr. Coyne interviews the partners separately and then brings them together for his summary and recommendations. This is his usual format.

Segment 2-5 – 2-7 Dr. Coyne asks Hugh for a small, specific example of his partner's annoying tendency to talk in vague and unclear ways. Hugh cites a conversation that occurred on the way to this interview in which his partner first said that they only had to put in one group of plants on their next job but then in the next breath referred to at least two other groups of plants that they would be using. Hugh first tried to clarify what Alan meant but then, rather than get into an argument, just dropped the subject. Dr. Coyne wondered if maybe Alan was "just thinking out loud."

Observation Questions:

1. How effective is Dr. Coyne in pinning down the specific sequences involved in the couple's complaints?

___

___

___

___

___

Allyn and Bacon Video Workshop: Family Therapy

2. What are the pros and cons of offering this couple therapy versus simply reinforcing the idea that they have already resolved their most pressing problems and perhaps don't need therapy at this point – or at least having that discussion with them?

3. On the other hand, what would be the advantages and disadvantages of exploring the more serious problems that Hugh alludes to but does not describe?

Segment 2-25 – 2-29 Alan agrees that he and Hugh sometimes have trouble communicating. He cites the fact that he tends to get very upset when Hugh expresses annoyance about something, even though it may have nothing to do with him. He tends to want to fix whatever the problem is, but that often isn't helpful. Dr. Coyne asks if there is a way for him not to take Hugh's anger so personally, but Alan says he can't help getting upset.

Observation Questions:

1. Does meeting with this partner second seem to have biased the content of their discussion?

2. How clearly has the therapist clarified Alan's complaint?

3. What are the pros and cons of the therapist's choice not to explore the roots of Alan's tendency to overreact to expressions of anger?

Allyn and Bacon Video Workshop: Family Therapy

Segment 2-40 – 2-43 *Dr. Coyne gives the couple a paradoxical assignment. Instead of continuing to try to change their two communication problems, the partners are just to notice when they occur and how they react. That is, Hugh is to continue occasionally getting irritable and Alan is to continue to overreact; while Alan is to continue to express himself vaguely ("to think out loud") and Hugh is to continue to try to pin him down.*

Observation Questions:

1. How effectively does the therapist "sell" this paradoxical directive?

2. Do the clients seem to understand clearly that they are to continue to enact their presenting complaints?

3. Do you think they will comply?

4. What do you expect they will report about this assignment when they come to their next therapy session?

Allyn and Bacon Video Workshop: Family Therapy

Solution-Oriented Therapy with Bill O'Hanlon

Brief Synopsis:

This family in this consultation consists of a husband (Adrian) and wife (Judy) and their 30-year-old daughter (Pam) who still lives at home. The parents complain that Pam doesn't communicate with them and that she has low self-esteem. She is dependent on them, but the price of that is that they are always full of criticism and advice. When she feels pushed, she retreats into silence or says "I don't know." Thus, her "not listening" is really a symptom of the rebellion of an adult child enmeshed with her controlling parents.

In this interview the therapist consistently looks for positives to build on, to which the parents consistently respond by brining up yet more complaints.

Segment 2-7 – 2-12 *The therapist drives to drive a wedge into the father's complain that his daughter clams up "all the time" by getting him to amend that to "ninety-nine percent of the time." "Tell me about that one percent," the therapist says. With the therapist's help, Pam describes a recent incident in which she got herself dressed and out of the house to attend a wake without her parents' nagging. "How did you get yourself to do that?" the therapist asks. He continues to express curiosity about how this exception came about.*

Observation Questions:

1. How effective is the therapist in shifting the parents from criticizing to recognizing Pam's capabilities?

_____
_____
_____
_____
_____
_____
_____

2. What's the main reason Pam was able to act responsibly in this incident? How effectively does the therapist develop this reason?

3. How differently does Pam respond to her parents? Why? How does the therapist work with this discrepancy?

4. To what extend does the therapist's focus on the positive in this example seem to plant the seed for change?

Allyn and Bacon Video Workshop: Family Therapy

Segment 2-30 – 2-37 *The therapist asks the family what can you do to make communication "just a little bit better." The parents respond by suggesting that Pam could not get angry at them. The therapist continues to work for a small solution and comes up with the suggestion that maybe Pam could say that she's angry when she feels pressured, rather than stomping off and banging things. Pam agrees to make this "one little change."*

Observation Questions:

1. To what extent do you think Pam has "yes-ed" the therapist just as she does with her parents?

_____
_____
_____
_____
_____
_____
_____
_____

2. Do you see constraints that stand in the way of Pam and her parents changing the patterns of interaction they complain of?

_____
_____
_____
_____
_____
_____
_____
_____

3. How necessary is it for a therapist to address these constraints?

4. What direct and indirect suggestions do you see the therapist making? Which are effective? Which less so?

5. How does the therapist show confidence in family members' abilities to change constructively? Is this confidence useful or misplaced?

Allyn and Bacon Video Workshop: Family Therapy

6. If the father, who is retired, is enmeshed with his daughter, how will this affect her ability to make friends outside the family? What some reasons for and against the necessity of addressing this structural arrangement?

_____
_____
_____
_____
_____
_____
_____
_____

Allyn and Bacon Video Workshop: Family Therapy

Object Relations Therapy with Drs. David and Jill Scharff

Brief Synopsis:

This family in this consultation consists of a husband (Adrian) and wife (Judy) and their 30-year-old daughter (Pam) who still lives at home. The parents complain that Pam doesn't communicate with them and that she has low self-esteem. She is dependent on them, but the price of that is that they are always full of criticism and advice. When she feels pushed, she retreats into silence or says "I don't know." Thus, her "not listening" is really a symptom of the rebellion of an adult child enmeshed with her controlling parents.

In this interview the therapists focus on the individual family members' feelings – expressed and avoided -- and uncover powerful unresolved feelings of grief over the suicide death of Pam's younger brother, Victor.

Segment 2-9 – 2-14 David Scharff asks Pam why she likes to sit between her parents – implying not just the seating arrangement but her role in the family. She feels "secure" being between her parents, though she is unable to say why. In this segment, it is revealed that Pam's younger brother, Victor, committed suicide when Pam was in community college. Pam was clearly very close to her brother, and, just as clearly, the family has avoided talking about this tragic loss.

Observation Questions:

1. What did the therapists do to uncover the family's suppressed grief over the loss of their son Victor?

_____
_____
_____
_____
_____
_____
_____
_____

2. To what extent does Pam grasp the therapist's suggestion that her role in the family comes between her parents?

3. Whether or not Pam consciously understands and accepts the implication that she comes between her parents, does this interpretation seem to open up significant material?

4. In this segment, how do you see these analytic therapists acting differently from how various other types of therapists might respond (e.g., do they offer support, reassurance, etc.)?

Allyn and Bacon Video Workshop: Family Therapy

Segment 2-38 –2-44 *David Scharff offers the tentative interpretation that keeping Pam at home may be a way of filling the void left by Victor's suicide. The father vigorously denies this suggestion. Later in this segment, Pam says that her anger comes from the fact that her parents won't let her alone to relax after she comes home from work but are always bugging her to do chores around the house.*

Observation Questions:

1. How accurate do you think the interpretation that Pam remains at home to fill the void left by Victor is?

2. What is the impact of this interpretation? How do all three family members respond? What effect does this interpretation have on the subsequent discussion?

Allyn and Bacon Video Workshop: Family Therapy

3. How do the therapists function together as a team? What advantages and disadvantages does having two therapists seem to make in this interview?

4. To what extent do you think Pam's closeness to her father represents an unresolved oedipal attachment?

5. How is the work in this interview similar and different to how a Bowenian or experiential therapist might proceed?

6. To what extent do you think that Pam's continuing to live at home with her parents can be seen as an arrested development due to a failure to move beyond the tragic death of her brother versus some kind of biological problem?

_____

_____

_____

_____

_____

_____

_____

_____

Allyn and Bacon Video Workshop: Family Therapy

Narrative Therapy with Dr. Steve Madigan

Brief Synopsis:

The clients in this session are an African-American mother and her son, who appears to be about thirteen. The boy was ordered to seek counseling by a juvenile court judge following an incident at school in which the boy, Ollie, hit another boy with his belt.

Madigan begins by eliciting first the boy's and then the mother's narrative account of what happened at school and at court. According to Ollie, he and the other boy were just fooling around, not really fighting. His mother agrees and says that the judge seriously overreacted. With a little prompting from the therapist, the mother says that she believes the incident was blown out of proportion because her son is black and the other child was white. The therapist sees no reason to question Ollie's account that the incident wasn't a real fight, and he is sympathetic to the mother's concern that school authorities are racist. Madigan ends by offering his support for the family, and he offers to write a letter to the school principal expressing his belief that Ollie is a good boy.

Segment 2-8 – 2-12 In this segment, the therapist elicits the clients' problem story and their "preferred views." Ollie's mother says that he is a good boy but when people aggravate him he loses his temper. Dr. Madigan explores with Ollie the possible future consequences of his developing a "troubled reputation" versus developing a "good-boy reputation." Ollie says that it's important to maintain a good reputation to stay out of trouble and to be successful in life.

Observation Questions:

1. Do you think Ollie believes that it's important to maintain a good reputation, or is he just saying what he thinks the white interviewer wants to hear?

_____
_____
_____
_____
_____
_____

2. Notice the therapist's use of persistent questions. To what extent does he seem to be following, versus leading, the clients?

Segment 2-13 – 2-16 In this segment, the therapist "externalizes" the problem, asking what would happen if "Trouble" started taking over Ollie's life. Ollie's mother says that it's important not to get a bad reputation.

Observation Questions:

1. Does this attempt at externalization seem to take? Do the clients follow the therapist's lead in defining the problem as an alien force?

Allyn and Bacon Video Workshop: Family Therapy

2. How effectively do you think the therapist is in "externalizing" the problem? How effectively does he accommodate to the family's response to his attempt?

___

Segment 2-19 – 2-22 *Dr. Madigan asks Ollie's mother if she knows why her son was treated in an overly punitive way for such a minor infraction. With a little prompting, the mother says that she thinks the school district isn't used to having black children and that they expect the worst of, especially male, black students.*

Observation Questions:

1. What is the effect of bringing out this point (that Ollie is a victim of racism)?

___

2. What are possible positive and negative consequences of attributing Ollie's problems with the judicial system to racism?

___

Allyn and Bacon Video Workshop: Family Therapy

3. To what extent does the therapist's sharing the mother's belief that the school authorities are racist reinforce or undermine the idea that Ollie must work hard to avoid developing a "troubled reputation?"

Segment 2-39 – 2-45 In this segment, the therapist tries to help the family consider ways to develop a supportive audience for Ollie's preferred story of himself – that is, that he is a good boy. Madigan even offers to write letters on Ollie's behalf. The mother responds that the school district should change its attitude. Dr. Madigan closes by offering to stay in touch with Ollie.

Observation Questions:

1. How effectively did the therapist explore possible supportive resources for Ollie's wish to be seen as a good boy? What other resources might he have suggested?

2. To what extent does the therapist' offer to stay in touch seem to fit the clients' needs and wishes?

3. Overall in this interview, the therapist accepts the family's description of events. What is lost and what is gained by so doing?

4. What possible problems or sources of conflict might the therapist have overlooked?

Allyn and Bacon Video Workshop: Family Therapy

Integrative Family Therapy with Dr. Ken Hardy

Brief Synopsis:

Dr. Hardy interviews an African-American single mother and her nineteen-year-old daughter, Erica. The mother begins by describing a recent incident in which, following an altercation with her boyfriend, Erica smashed his car window with a baseball bat and then went into the house to get a kitchen knife. It was at that point that her mother intervened. The mother describes her daughter as a "high-maintenance" child and says that the two of them have had a lot of conflict. She sees her daughter as "fragile" (meaning emotionally reactive).

When Dr. Hardy asks Erica for her view of the blow-up with her boyfriend, she changes the subject to her relationship with her mother, complaining that her mother isn't very understanding or supportive.

Hardy spends the remainder of the session discussing the mother and daughter's relationship and encourages the mother to see that her daughter needs more closeness and attention from her.

Segment 2-16 – 2-20 Dr. Hardy asks Erica to tell her mother directly what she wants from her, and he asks the mother to just listen. Erica talks about feeling hurt that her mother wasn't more helpful in teaching her to drive so that she could get a driver's license. She also says that her mother has often been unwilling to talk with her about her personal issues and problems. She wishes her mother would respect her more and be proud of her.

Observation Questions:

1. To what extent does Dr. Hardy's having Erica express her feelings to her mother seem like an "enactment" a la structural family therapy or more of a technique drawn from some other model of therapy?

_____
_____
_____
_____
_____

Allyn and Bacon Video Workshop: Family Therapy

2. What does this conversation accomplish?

3. What is the process and what is the content of this conversation?

4. What are the advantages and disadvantages of Dr. Hardy's asking the mother not to respond but just to listen to her daughter's complaints?

Allyn and Bacon Video Workshop: Family Therapy

Segment 2-26 – 2-30 *This time Dr. Hardy asks the mother to explain to her daughter why she wasn't more helpful in her getting a driver's license. When the mother tries to explain her reasons, Dr. Hardy interrupts what looks to be the start of a familiar quarrel to ask the mother to express some appreciation of her daughter's disappointment. The mother does acknowledge her daughter's disappointment but adds that she worried that she might get into an accident because she was so irresponsible. Dr. Hardy tries hard to make this sound more like loving concern than lack of trust. Erica counters her mother's explanations by saying that "she is just making up excuses."*

Observation Questions:

1. To what extent does Dr. Hardy's controlling and shaping the conversation work effectively to improve the relationship between mother and daughter?

_____
_____
_____
_____
_____
_____
_____
_____

2. To what extent does Dr. Hardy's controlling and shaping the conversation interfere with working on the relationship between mother and daughter?

_____
_____
_____
_____
_____
_____
_____
_____

Allyn and Bacon Video Workshop: Family Therapy

3. To what extent does the therapist seem to be inducted into treating this nineteen-year-old woman as a child in need of more understanding and nurture from her mother? What are the advantages and disadvantages of his taking this approach?

_____
_____
_____
_____
_____
_____
_____
_____

Segment 2-31 – 2-38 Dr. Hardy suggests that Erica show anger when she feels hurt. Erica denies this and says that she doesn't feel hurt. Then Dr. Hardy offers the interpretation that not obtaining a driver's license is a way for Erica to remain dependent on her mother. The mother agrees, but Dr. Hardy reframes this as a wish for closeness rather than dependency.

Dr. Hardy points out to the mother that her thinking of her daughter as "fragile" and "co-dependent," implying that she should be strong and grow up, has the effect of pushing her away.

Observation Questions:

1. To what extent do mother and daughter seem to accept Dr. Hardy's interpretation of their relationship?

_____
_____
_____
_____
_____
_____
_____
_____

2. What are the advantages and disadvantages of his lengthy comments?

3. What evidence is there that the distinction between describing Erica as "sensitive" versus "fragile" is substantive rather than semantic? That is, does the mother come to changer her perception of her daughter or just accept the therapist's use of a different term?

4. What is gained and what is lost by not exploring the daughter's having used a baseball bat and a knife in her argument with her boyfriend? If you see this as avoiding conflict on the therapist's part, what would explain his having done that?

Allyn and Bacon Video Workshop: Family Therapy

5. Do you see the work in this session as having integrated various approaches? If so, which ones?

_____
_____
_____
_____
_____
_____
_____
_____

6. What are the impacts of race and gender in this interview?

_____
_____
_____
_____
_____
_____
_____
_____

Allyn and Bacon Video Workshop: Family Therapy

Imago Therapy with Dr. Pat Love

Brief Synopsis:

Dave and Cathy are a young married couple who are having problems communicating. He wishes they could talk without getting into big arguments, and she wishes they could talk more. Partly because the therapist is so active in initiating structured exercises and partly because the couple, especially the husband, are fairly defensive, their complaints don't get fully clarified. However, they appear to have a pursuer-distancer pattern in which Cathy tries to get Dave to tell her everything that's going on, while he is somewhat reticent for fear that she will criticize and complain.

Through much of the session, Dr. Love uses a "mirroring" technique, a structured exercise in which one partner talks while the other listens without comment and then paraphrases what was said. Using this device, the partners are able to talk without arguing, but it isn't clear that their complaints were fully explored or that they learned anything about how to communicate on their own.

Segment 2-9 – 2-12 The therapist asks each of the partners to say how they contribute to the couple's communication problems. Dave says that he tends to bottle up complaints. When Dr. Love asks him how he feels when he holds things in, he talks vaguely about being concerned about how Cathy might respond if he were more open. Dr. Love then asks Cathy to paraphrase what she heard Dave saying.

Observation Questions:

1. How clearly does Dave express why he's afraid to open up to his wife?

_____
_____
_____
_____
_____
_____
_____
_____

2. How does the process of what occurs in this segment mirror the content?

3. How well does Cathy succeed in paraphrasing why her husband hesitates to open up to her?

4. How successfully do you think this mirroring technique is here in getting the couple to understand how each other feels?

Allyn and Bacon Video Workshop: Family Therapy

Segment 2-18 – 2-20 *Dr. Love asks Dave what his wife could do to show more acceptance of him. He responds by saying that he would like her to compliment him more often.*

Observation Questions:

1. What is the implicit complaint behind Dave's request?

2. How effectively is this issue dealt with?

3. Does Cathy seem to understand what she does that bothers her husband?

Allyn and Bacon Video Workshop: Family Therapy

Segment 2-28 -- 2-32 *When Dr. Love asks Cathy what she does to contribute to the couple's communication problems, she replies that she asks too many questions. She does that, she says, because she wants Dave to be more open with her.*

Observation Questions:

1. Why does Cathy asks her husband so many questions? What are the implications of seeing this as: (a) merely a wish for more communication or (b) an expression of lack of trust?

___

2. As a result of this exercise, do you think that Cathy thinks she should grill her husband less or that he should be more open with her? In other words, is this device effective in helping her see something that she can change?

___

Segment 2-35 – 2-39 *Dr. Love asks Dave why he hesitates to tell Cathy things. He says that he's afraid that it will look like he failed. When Dr. Love asks Cathy what she thinks she does that contributes to Dave's reticence, she says that she grills him with questions.*

Allyn and Bacon Video Workshop: Family Therapy

Observation Questions:

1. What is implied when Dave says that he hesitates to tell his wife things for fear that it will look like he failed? Why is he so indirect?

2. How could a therapist help him be more direct?

3. What is helpful and what is unhelpful about the therapists extreme level of activity and control?

4. What do you think each of the partners realize as a result of this intervention? What do they fail to realize?

Allyn and Bacon Video Workshop: Family Therapy

Empowerment Therapy with Dr. Frank Pittman

Brief Synopsis:

(Rather than being a particular model or school of thought, "empowerment therapy" is merely a name Frank Pittman came up with for his integrative approach to working with couples and families.)

Tom and Susan are a couple in their mid-thirties. It is her first marriage; his second. They have three children, two of their own and his ten-year-old daughter from his first marriage. The presenting problem is that they argue all the time. According to Tom, Susan is always pestering him to do things. Her complaint is that he won't talk with her, and when he does, he starts shouting. She also says that she needs more help around the house and with the children.

Dr. Pittman explores their complaints, asks each of them about the model of the families the grew up in, and spends much of the interview expressing empathy for Tom's feeling that nothing he does is good enough.

Segment 2-23 – 2-28 In this segment, Dr. Pittman asks Susan to try to understand how Tom feels powerless and put upon. "He doesn't feel that he has a voice." He goes on to suggest that since Tom is trying to be a better father (especially better than how own alcoholic and abusive father) he should talk with Susan's father about how to be a good father. Pittman suggests that Tom grew up without a father because "drunks don't count."

Observation Questions:

1. How well does Susan appear to hear and accept the therapist's suggestion that she try harder to understand how her husband feels?

_____
_____
_____
_____
_____
_____

Allyn and Bacon Video Workshop: Family Therapy

2. What might be necessary to do before the wife feels more like listening to the husband?

3. How do each of the partners respond to the therapist's interventions in this segment?

4. How fair and balanced does the therapist show himself to be?

5. What is the effect of the therapist say in reference to Tom's father that "drunks don't count"?

_____
_____
_____
_____
_____
_____
_____
_____

6. What do you think of the suggestion that Tom should talk to his father-in-law about how to be a better father? (Might learning to talk with his father-in-law make it easier for him to talk to his wife?)

_____
_____
_____
_____
_____
_____
_____
_____
_____
_____

Segment 2-28 – 2-32 Dr. Pittman suggests that instead of waiting for Susan to tell him what to do and then feeling put upon and defensive that Tom should take the initiative to get more involved. Moreover, the therapist suggests that the couple should talk more about what to do?

Observation Questions:

1. What do you think of the suggestion that Tom start taking the initiative instead of remaining in a passive and reactive position?

_____
_____
_____

2. What might make it difficult for Tom to follow this advice? For Susan to let him?

3. What might the suggestion that the couple talk more together about what to do accomplish?

4. What does this suggestion overlook?

Segment 2-38 – 2-44 Dr. Pittman offers the interpretation that Tom defends himself from his wife's entreaties as though someone were abusing him – as his father did physically, and his ex-wife did emotionally. His primary way of defending himself against a feared attack is by not talking. Pittman goes on to tell Susan that she won't be able to get close to Tom if she overwhelms him with criticisms and complaints. According to Dr. Pittman, Tom resists Susan to protect himself from feeling dominated.

Dr. Pittman again urges Tom to talk with his father-in-law about being a father, and when Tom says that he isn't sure that would want to be a father according to what his father-in-law tells him, Dr. Pittman makes the very useful point that "just talking doesn't mean that you have to do what he says."

Observation Questions:

1. What might Susan gain if she accepts Dr. Pittman's interpretation that Tom defends himself because he fears being attacked?

2. To what extent do you think that Susan accepts what Dr. Pittman is saying?

3. How balanced is the therapist's stance?

4. Must a therapist be even-handed? What happens if he or she isn't?

5. How might you intervene to get through to Susan?

6. What do you think Tom needs to change? To what extent will this interview help him see a way for him to behave differently?

7. Do you think that Tom grasps the implication that just as he can talk with his father-in-law without having to do what he says, he can also talk with his wife without having to do what she says?

Allyn and Bacon Video Workshop: Family Therapy

Adlerian Therapy with Dr. James Bitter

Brief Synopsis:

The clients in this family are a working-class couple and their three, pre-teenage children. In what appears to be a very educational approach to working with families, Dr. Bitter structures and controls the session by asking everyone in turn a series of questions, many of which appear to be standard – such as, for example, asking the family to describe a typical day. The first time he addresses the parents, he asks them to choose three adjectives to describe their children. He talks with the children as much as the with parents, and in fact opens the session by talking with the middle child.

The presenting complain is express by the mother who says that she wants the children to listen more, especially the older two, Michael and Andrea. She goes on to say that when she does try to discipline the children, her husband will often interfere and tell her to stop yelling at them. She also complains that her own mother and sister, who live nearby, interfere with her discipline.

Segment 2-18 –2-24 Dr. Bitter asks the family to describe a typical day, which they do. In the process, the mother complains mildly about the children's behavior.

Observation Questions:

1. What are the advantages and disadvantages of the therapist's controlling the interview to the extent that he does?

_____
_____
_____
_____
_____
_____
_____

Allyn and Bacon Video Workshop: Family Therapy

2. What might be gained by having the parents discuss with each other their differences about parenting? What might be lost?

___

3. Do the children seem to feel free to interrupt their parents? What does this suggest about the family structure? How does the therapist respond?

___

Segment 2-26 – 2-29 The therapist asks the mother what purpose she thinks the children have for not listening to her? She doesn't know. He then offers the interpretation that not listening to her is her children's way of dealing with her needing everything to be done just right. And, he adds, it also enables the children to remain dependent on her.

Observation Questions:

1. How accurate are these interpretations? Do they appear to emerge from the specific material in this session, or do they appear to be generic comments?

___

Allyn and Bacon Video Workshop: Family Therapy

2. What impact do these interpretations appear to have on various family members?

3. Does the first part of the interpretation appear to elevate the children at their mother's expense?

Segment 2-30 – 2-35 In this segment Dr. Bitter offers his summary comments and recommendations. He tells the parents that their problems are perfectly normal. But he advises the father to: (1) stop interfering when his wife is disciplining the children, and (2) work out an agreement with her in which they take turns dealing with the children – e.g., if one gets them ready for school, the other will get them ready for bed. To the mother, Dr. Bitter recommends that she stop nagging the children and start taking action. He also tells the parents to stop doing things for the children that they can do for themselves – such as wake up and get ready for school in the morning.

Observation Questions:

1. Which of these pieces of advise do you think the family will follow, and which not?

_____
_____
_____
_____
_____
_____
_____
_____

2. Why haven't the parents already put these common-sense ideas into practice? Is it simply a matter of ignorance or is there more to it?

_____
_____
_____
_____
_____
_____
_____
_____

3. What are the advantages of this kind of educational approach?

_____
_____
_____
_____
_____
_____
_____
_____

Allyn and Bacon Video Workshop: Family Therapy

4. What are the limits of a strictly educational approach?

_____
_____
_____
_____
_____
_____
_____
_____

5. If the mother feels a need to have everything done right (according to her standards), why would the therapist's suggesting she stop work?

_____
_____
_____
_____
_____
_____
_____
_____

6. Can you see any conflicts that might not have been dealt with in this interview?

_____
_____
_____
_____
_____
_____
_____
_____

Allyn and Bacon Video Workshop: Family Therapy

Emotionally Focused Couples Therapy with Dr. Susan Johnson

Brief Synopsis:

Scott and Leslie are a married couple with children who appear to be in their late thirties. They have recently separated and, although Scott wants to get back together, Leslie is reluctant to take him back until he does something about his bad temper. As she puts it, she wants him "to act like more of an adult." But she's been asking him to do something about his temper for years, and he hasn't. Scott admits that he has a bad temper, although he seems somehow proud of it, almost as though having a temper were his way of reassuring himself that he's powerful. What makes him especially angry is when he blows up at one of the children and his wife steps in to tell him to calm down.

Dr. Johnson spends most of the session probing for what she thinks the partners' attachment issues are: wanting to feel safe and connected, and not wanting to be abandoned. Most of her dialogue is with Scott, but while he listens respectfully, neither he nor his wife appear to have much of an emotional experience. Scott doesn't appear ready to give up his anger and doesn't really see why he "should cry in front of his wife." Leslie doesn't really get beyond restated that Scott should control her temper, and no attempt is made to point our her role in the dysfunctional pattern.

Segment 2-4 –2-7 Leslie says that she's been asking Scott to do something about his temper for years, but he hasn't, and so she no longer trusts him. The two of them regularly get into huge arguments, especially when Leslie steps in to defend the children against Scott's anger.

Observation Questions:

1. Given that Scott acknowledges his temper but doesn't seem really to be ashamed of it (in fact he seems almost proud of it), what feelings might his displays of temper be defending against? How might you explore this issue?

_____
_____
_____
_____

Allyn and Bacon Video Workshop: Family Therapy

2. What is the effect of treating an emotion, such as anger, as something that should be controlled without exploring what makes that person angry? Is more control the answer?

3. If communication has two levels: content and metacommunication (an attempt to define the relationship in a certain way), what is the metacommunication in Leslie's telling Scott that he should control his temper?

4. How would you address the issue that Scott seems to feel that Leslie treats him like a child? Why might he actually want that kind of relationship with her?

Allyn and Bacon Video Workshop: Family Therapy

_____
_____

Segment 2-16 – 2-24 In this segment, Scott acknowledges that he has a bad temper, saying "I'm a mean and nasty kind of guy." But he laughs when he says this about himself, almost as though he were proud of it. But the therapist continues to probe for attachment feelings. She asks him if he is afraid that that (mean and nasty) is how his wife sees him. Then she asks him if he feels rejected.

The therapist asks Scott if he thinks that Leslie understands how he feels when she criticizes him. He says she doesn't care how he feels; she denies this. The therapist continues to probe for feelings of hurt behind the couple's conflict.

Observation Questions:

1. What complex set of attitudes does Scott seem to have about his temper?

_____
_____
_____
_____
_____
_____
_____
_____

2. What is the effect of talking about Scott's temper as alien ("it's not you, it's your temper") have on helping him (and his wife) develop more understanding – of what provokes him, what he's afraid of, why he feels the need to erect a façade of strength, etc.

_____
_____
_____
_____
_____
_____
_____

Allyn and Bacon Video Workshop: Family Therapy

_____
_____

3. What is the opposite of the show of angry strength that Scott portrays? How much you explore for the possible existence of such feelings without making him even more defensive?

_____
_____
_____
_____
_____
_____
_____
_____

4. Why might this couple have chosen each other? How would you explore that?

_____
_____
_____
_____
_____
_____
_____
_____

5. How might you begin to point out to Leslie her role in the couple's dysfunctional pattern?

_____
_____
_____
_____
_____

6. If effective therapy involves insight and emotional experience, which needs to come first? Does that appear to happen in this session?

NOTES

NOTES

NOTES

NOTES

NOTES